Grandpa and Me and
the Wishing Star

Dedicated with love to
Walter C. Johnson
and Lyman K. Porter

©1990 Deseret Book Company

Library of Congress Catalog Card No. 90-81831

ISBN 0-87579-269-3

Printed in the United States of America

10   9   8   7   6   5   4   3   2

Grandpa and Me and the Wishing Star

Written by
Barbara J. Porter
Illustrated by
Dilleen Marsh

Deseret Book Company
Salt Lake City, Utah

Grandpa and I were best friends. In the spring-time, we took long walks and looked for robins and counted how many trees had buds on them. We laughed and told jokes. Grandpa always thought my jokes were funny, even when no one else did. Sometimes Grandpa talked about the things he did when he was my age. Then he rumpled my hair and said, "Who's my best boy?"

And I said, "I am."

In the summer, Grandpa and I walked in the mountains. Sometimes we sat by a creek and threw rocks in the water. If we found a still pool, we watched the ripples get bigger and bigger. Once I asked Grandpa how big the circle would get if we dropped a rock from an airplane.

Grandpa thought for a long time. Finally he said, "Jamie, I don't know the answer to that. But I do know that people who ask questions usually find more answers than people who don't. When you find the answer to that one, you let me know."

I said I would.

Then he rumpled my hair and said, "Who's my best boy?"

And I said, "I am."

On autumn evenings, Grandpa and I looked up at the sky. We had one special star that was the very brightest. Grandpa said it was a wishing star, and when we saw it, we each made a wish. We never told each other what we wished — if you tell, the wish won't come true.

Sometimes on those evenings, Grandpa got a far-away look in his eyes. I wondered if he was thinking about Grandma. Grandma died when I was just little, and I thought maybe Grandpa's wish had something to do with her, but I never asked him. Anyway, pretty soon he looked at me and smiled. Then he said, "Who's my best boy?"

And I said, "I am."

In the wintertime, Grandpa and I sat by the fire. If you watch the flames long enough, you can see pictures in them. Grandpa read to me, and we ate apples. Grandpa cut his into tiny pieces and took a long time to eat it because he didn't have his real teeth anymore. "It's tough to be old, Jamie," he said, "especially when you can't eat apples."

I said, "You're not old, Grandpa."

He laughed and tickled me, and I tickled him back, and we kept laughing and tickling until we could hardly breathe. Then when Grandpa finally caught his breath, he said, "Who's my best boy?"

And I said, "I am."

One day, I stopped at Grandpa's house on my way home from school. An ambulance was in the driveway. My mom was standing on the lawn, and they were carrying Grandpa out of the house on a stretcher. Mom held me tight and said they were taking Grandpa to the hospital. Mom went with him, but I had to go home and stay with my little sister.

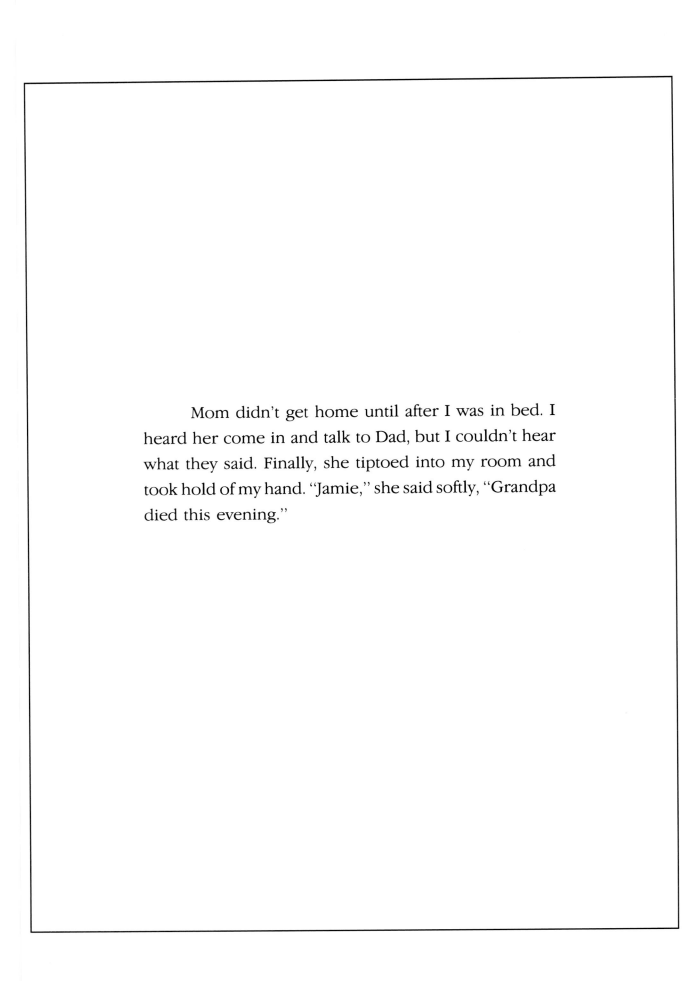

Mom didn't get home until after I was in bed. I heard her come in and talk to Dad, but I couldn't hear what they said. Finally, she tiptoed into my room and took hold of my hand. "Jamie," she said softly, "Grandpa died this evening."

"*No!*" I shouted. I pulled my hand away and held my pillow tight over my ears so I couldn't hear her. She sat on my bed for a while, stroking my arm. I think she was crying, but I didn't uncover my head to see.

Finally she whispered, "He's happy, Jamie. He's with Grandma now." Then she kissed me and left the room. I lay there for a long time, cold and empty inside.

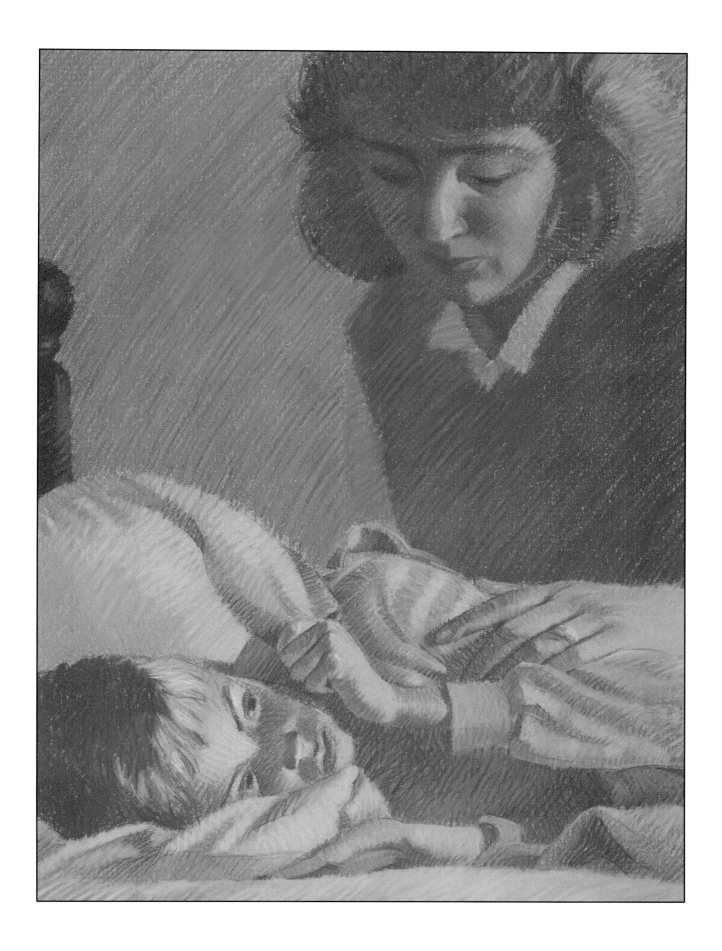

The next day, Mom was gone a lot. After dinner, Dad and Mom called my sisters and me into the living room. They talked to us about Heavenly Father and Jesus, and we sang "Families Can Be Together Forever." They said how happy Grandma and Grandpa must be now. I'd heard all that stuff before, and I knew it was true, but that didn't make me stop hurting inside. I didn't want Grandpa to be in heaven with Grandma. I wanted him to be with me, looking for robins and throwing rocks in the pond and wishing on our star.

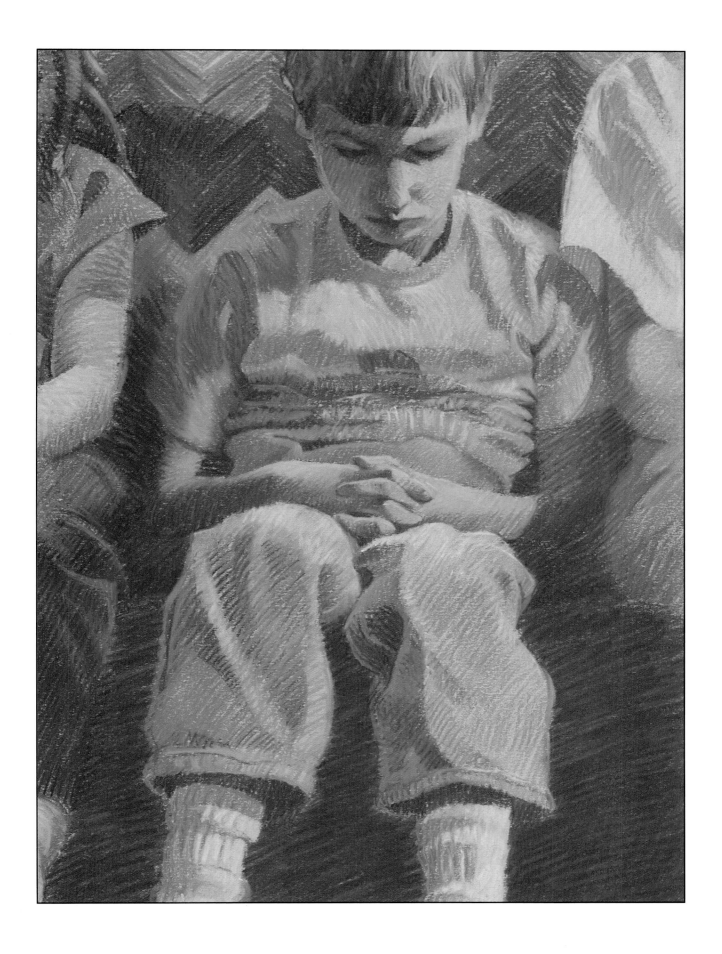

Mom and Dad said the funeral was nice. I didn't think it was. All the grandchildren had to sing, "I Am a Child of God," but I didn't feel like singing. Everybody said how nice Grandpa looked, but I didn't think he did. I thought he looked white and cold and dead.

When we finally came home, I went to my room and didn't come out. Mom came up and said, "Won't you come and eat something, Jamie? Your cousins are all here."

I just looked out the window and didn't answer her. She came over, put her arm around me, and said, "I know you miss Grandpa. I miss him too." When I looked down, I saw tears dropping onto the window sill, but they weren't mom's tears—they were mine. Mom held me tight until I finally stopped crying. Then she handed me a kleenex and smiled. "Do you think you could come downstairs now?"

I said, "No."

She kissed me and said, "Just come when you're ready."

That night, I said my prayers. I was almost afraid to. I thought Heavenly Father might be mad because I wasn't happy that Grandpa was with him. I tried to explain how I felt, and I told Heavenly Father that I hoped he understood. Then I lay in my bed and thought about Grandpa. I thought about the wishing star, and I wondered if now Grandpa's wish had come true.

I was almost asleep when a soft warm feeling came over me. It felt as if someone was tucking me in, like Mom did sometimes. I slowly opened my eyes, almost afraid the feeling would go away, but it was still there. I knelt on my bed and looked out the window. There was the wishing star. It looked brighter than I had ever seen it.

I made a wish. Then I snuggled back into bed. I felt safe and warm. In my mind, I heard Grandpa say, "Who's my best boy?"

I smiled to myself as I pulled the covers tight around me and whispered, "I am."